Bury Me Like This

———

Melissa Enslin

To every me in every state;

I know you're out there.

Scream joyfully into the void,

And hear this echo.

ISBN: 978-0-7961-7350-8 (E-Book)
ISBN: 978-0-7961-7349-2 (Hardcover)

Any references to historical events, real people, or real places are used fictitiously. Names, characters, and places are products of the author's imagination.

Front cover image is an extraction from a photograph taken by the author.
Photographs and edits thereof are by the author.
Book cover and design by the author.
Printed by Kindle Direct Publishing.com; ISBNs issued by the National Library of South Africa.

First printing edition 2024.
Melissa Enslin
menslin.writes@gmail.com

...I (read this in) bits at a time because it is hitting parts of my soul that have always needed words put to it. In a good way. We all go through different things but at the end of the day the effect on us is the same. I'm a soul on a human journey just like everybody else.

- Jodi-Lyn Shipton

Acknowledgements

Many people have impacted me in ways that led to each poem, but a few people have had a real hand in helping me get this collection off the ground.

Firstly, my wonderful partner and husband who not only lovingly read the book start to finish the very moment I was ready to share it, but who also endured my shortcomings when it came to format and graphics. Along with valuable perspective, he gave me space to make all the silly mistakes, and then he gave me his time and skills as he corrected each one without judgement when I finally stopped being stubborn. I hope you know what you bring to my life.

Secondly, my beautiful friend, whose words begin this book, for her encouragement that it was relevant and her input along the way. Our conversations are priceless to me.

To family, friends who have been like family, and anyone who has moulded me through hardness or flow, I see you and I thank you.

Mom, your journey enables my journey.

Mostly, I acknowledge the Spirit that moves in me and gives rise to seeing the world as I do. It is a Spirit that conflicts with the world as it is and has often left me feeling isolated; but it is also the same Spirit that has led me here, and here is beautiful.

A different kind of acknowledgement would be to put forward that where some language, imagery, or descriptions might seem offensive or off kilter to some: we don't walk each other's journeys but we can invest in understanding. Ask the Spirit.

Preface

A lecturer once explained poetry to our class as language under pressure (thanks, Dan Wylie). It stayed with me forever, and mutated in my understanding as an attempt to capture moments that are extremely hard to describe but that connect us to one another, or to all other things, or pierce right through us.

In that way, these poems speak to moments where I was experiencing extreme lucidity over something otherwise mundane or not especially important. These moments grew me. Or rather, they stretched my soul, because they didn't particularly make me more likely to succeed in the world's terms. But they did make me realise how much of what I felt on the daily had nothing to do with my human experience. They were my soul reaching through my senses and helping my human side grapple with why I may be here, as a soul, in the first place.

When I was teaching high school poetry, I really fell in love. Even though I had written and felt poetry for as long as I could remember, and even though I had studied literature, and then studied how to teach literature, it was only in those early years of teaching that I truly grasped the full concept of poetry being so precise – so intentional. I mean, really every little detail could be turned over. And then I understood how important it was to live and live and live through the thing you were trying to describe. It's a different language; it's of the soul. And so when trying to figure out what to say in these few lines, it felt so strange because the *poems* are how I want to connect. What could I say *here* to connect with you, to make you want to read these things. I don't want to try and flesh out, in an everyday form of speech, why these poems will reach you.

If you are here already, I truly believe that you know two things: that poetry speaks to you because it is so infinite and finite in a way that prose never could be: a fish lens of experience in the sense that it aligns so much of what seems out of accord in this world; and then also that you will find an echo of yourself in these lines.

When this collection, written over so many years, finally came together, I was overwhelmed with relief. All the chaos and noise and oddities finally made sense, and more than that, it felt light.

I could speak about each poem at length — how some of them allude to great poems of the past, or widely publicised events. But each will, and should, resonate differently to anyone who reads them. We all have versions of ourselves that we are reaching to be, or trying our hardest not to be. We have our ways we feel stuck and ways we feel free. One poem may have been my anchor while it is your elation. And so it should be. So I won't invest energy into deciphering any of them here. They were mine in the moments they rolled out of me, but if you are reading this, they are yours now, and you can turn them over however you want.

The poems are already something different to me each time, as though each one sums up so many moments, each element so ambiguous and direct, that they will be what they are to each of you.

Perhaps I will take a moment to say that the photos, however unprofessional or obscure, were also moments of magnitude in the mundane that I was trying to capture, and that they sat beautifully alongside the words in my head and the smile in my soul enough to make it here as well.

I knew this would get away from me. I need to leave it to the poems now.

If there is one thought with which I'd like to stir your spirit before you turn the page, though, it is this:

Intention is everything, and it will colour your life more than anything else. Intend to see the beauty and feel the spirit and look to things as a child would, before the world started colouring in with its shadow.

CONTENTS

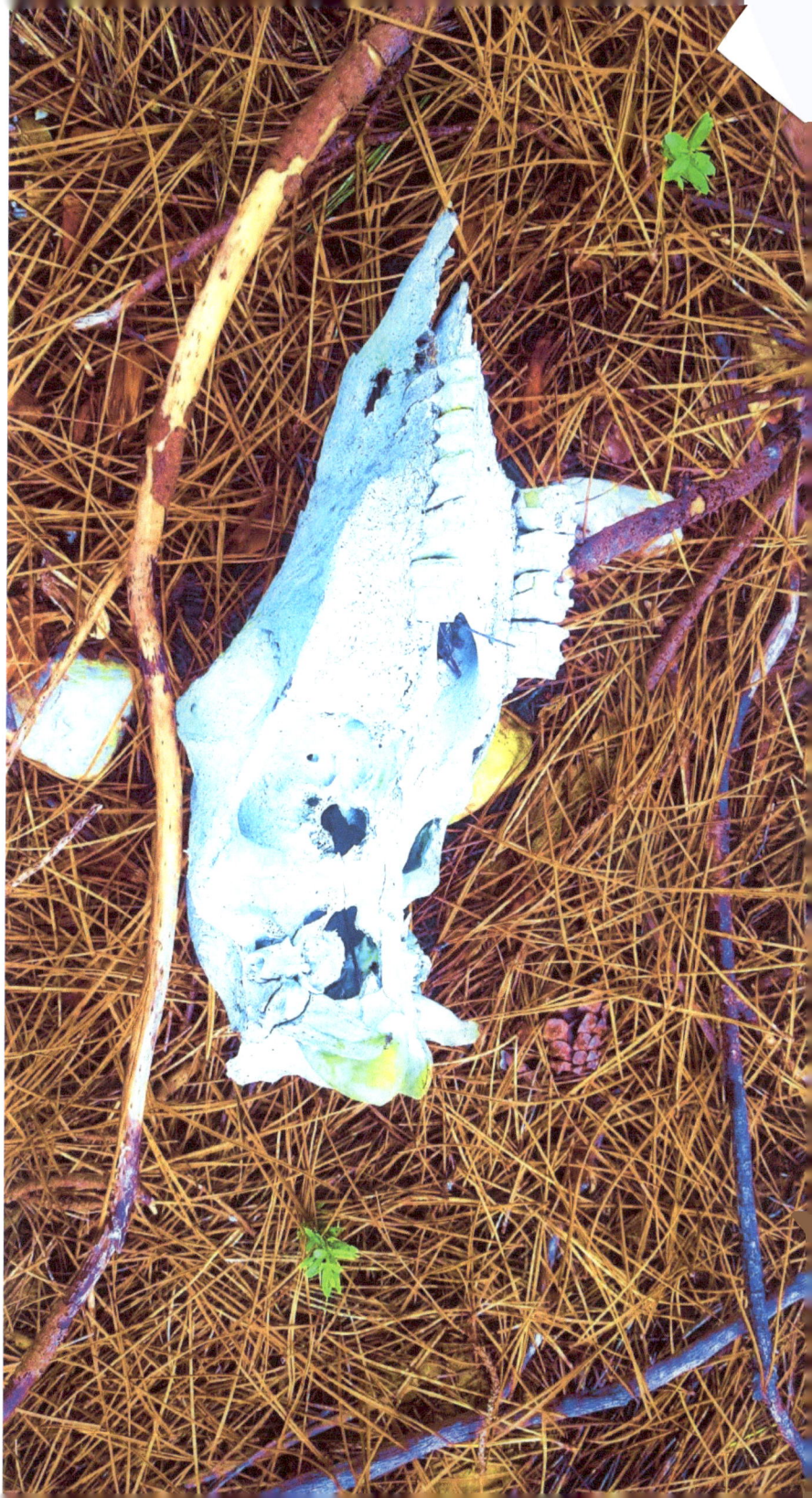

CHAPTER 1: ENDINGS

Baptism

A piercing of light through the haze
That moment that scales fall
and truth is absorbed like serum into the mind -
A heart grabbing hold of sense once more;
a jolt of anticipated torment
in this kind of truth
that doesn't come -
A flush of serenity in its place
is wondrous release from shackled confusion
When the fire dies...
The smoke is freed
from searing flames
that eat at it
and drifts upwards -
Light as calm -
To live among air,
Taking all the breaths it could want,
Shivering off the flaking ashes
Of a shell that needed burning.

Disappearing act

When all the world turns quiet -
Noise dies, people fade, energy stills -
Those who are part of your solitude
are those who are part of your soul.
In all the mayhem caused in crowds,
of fuzzy fumes and mingled tempers,
you may be swept up believing
a fairytale of words woven in trust
that are woven with nothing more
than cotton strands instead of silk.

They'll come apart.

And then you'll come apart.
Look for who stays when even you,
in part, disappear...

Root to tip

We have been emerging from the depths of the earth
In screams
Ever since the tremors came
And went
And been bathed in light so bright
That we have only just begun to try and
Look at it,
And the blood -
So much blood -
And tearing of flesh

And the *beingness* of everything,

Rushing through us
As though we are the wind,
The water,
The licking of flames…
Nothing was a metaphor -
No scripture
No message
No prophecy.

No dreams,

Images,

Nor miracles -

All of it was more real and striking

Than

everything

Everything

up until this

Was a murmur -

Muffled sounds and sights through screens,

A display to which we stood so close

that never before could its truth be gauged -

It had all been just a game.

A glint in the eye

Before something wild

Born of boredom

And challenge -

That fierceness that could not be put down.

I was heavy, trapped under the weight of

Truths I wanted to unlive -

unexperience and unfeel -
And suddenly I did.

In earthquakes that ripped the body open,
Spilling awful truths in front of me,
Like death - that must be
Death
and judgement
Because I wept

And couldn't look. And could not look away.
And then it all made sense –

Not in the way of joy,
But like a sunflower turning its head to the sun;
knowing the roots would always be there,
not trying to unbecome a root,
I knew.

Stop

Okay…
Focus…
There's too much "now"
And not enough foresight -
There's too much want
And not enough me;
Too much addiction
And not enough shape -
Desire takes away my goals
Makes me see less of where I'm going -
Stop.
Breathe.
Look at how to get there,
how to go.
I can only have you
if I keep me, now.
I'll know how to have you then
If I stay with me now;
in every now.
I would absorb into you, if I could,
With this hollow breath in this thought.

Mirror

I lost myself in you
And you were an inky abyss -
A bottomless pit -
Of nothing real
and I stayed too long;
Stared too long -
At the same spot of light
I thought I saw
In your face
Looking up
From where I'd fallen -
to notice
that it was a reflection of me;
Of my desire
For you
To be light -
To realise how stuck I was
in the base
of what you really were.

I still don't see my own light

Here
But now I am careful
not to see it in others -
And everything has gone dark.
I don't blame you -
I wish I didn't blame me,
Either.

Flight

Falling through the universe has
A funny way
Of making everything else lose momentum -
It simply ceases, no longer satisfies...
You can be flying a hundred miles an hour
doing almost anything
Else
But
Once your body has twirled in space
It just doesn't *feel* like
real movement anymore.
And then, where to go for the thrill
When you haven't yet
Realised
That this hole in the outer
Matter
Doesn't just happen accidentally
When trauma strikes
Or love hitchhikes...
It's not like that at all
Where the experience depends

On things you think

You don't control

It's more true to say that these things didn't come looking for you;

That you felt them while you were out looking for the dose

That gets you there

Because your soul

Is already addicted to it -

It comes from there;

That feeling is home

It's the one you can incite:

Draw in…

Hone.

CHAPTER 2: WHAT LIES BEHIND

Outside, inside, outside; done

Sitting at my desk

Stuck in a box

Boxed in

Looking at the box

Screen lit

Bright

Killing my eyes

Tired eyes

Concentration fading fast

Wondering why I couldn't just do

What I wanted with my life

Like be outside

Moving all the time

Doing stuff

Figuring out the world

Exploring

Making waves in the air

Instead of stuffing airwaves

But no -

I'm boxed in

Stuffy spaces

Forgetting faces
Of creatures too small
To see from inside.

Trade route

I used to do everything in heels
Now I always have dirty feet
And it's not because I gave up -
Just gave up going anywhere involving streets.
I cannot trade the sandy ground
Or grassy thorny slopes
For tiles or concrete,
Or a city-life kind of space.

Heard

There she sits in the glory seat
where we win and lose -
today's gladiator;
armoured by a social cause -
mushroomed voices;
A face for all our faces.
Throne entombed.
Not quite ready for the strum;
for the thumb of truth to fall;
A penny, for what it can change.

Quiet settles -
Like an ember's cackle.

Is she me?
I've never done anything like this before...
but she is me.
Waiting for the guillotine;
A mirage for all the things
we hope are never seen
or heard.

Our secret thoughts,
A synapsis for wicked acts.
And now this:
A stoned sacrifice
Of an amber lamb.

How hard, if at all,
Does her heart pound in that chair?
How *unlike* me is she, in truth?
Or is she just like me:
terrified of either truth being true?
Angry that both are?
She wears the darkness of power
first grabbed at in the heartbeat. Then,
accumulated silently,
overnight.
Wishes granted.
The fruits enjoyed.

Now, the wind peels away the forest -
mycelium exposed;
a drained basin
waiting for understanding

to happen,
either way;
hoping,
but refusing to pray.

There she sits,
awaiting the bell.
Her wishes granted,
the outcome obscene.

The fog shifts;
she gulps the scene.
Drug haze clearing.
Power becoming what it's always been.
On a boy, on a girl; woman or a man.
She'd just never seen it out the shadows before,
but now she's won the tug of war,
and the cost to bear
Won't escape us at all.

Intent

She came to work

She came to work wearing her badge

She came to work wearing her badge of bravery, of honour

She came to work as a leader

She came to work for respect

She came to work despite it all

She came to work

She came to work and passed on knowledge

She came to work and passed on knowledge, passed on death

She came to work and passed on death

She came to work

She came to work without a care

She came to work despite it all

She came to work

She came to work with death; gave it as a gift

She came to work without a test

She came to work without reading

She came to work without understanding

She came to work with assumptions

She came to work with the best intentions

She came to work with ignorance

She came to work and stamped in ignorance

She came to work

She came to work brave

She came to work strong

She came to work with the best intentions

She came to work despite it all

She came to work and killed them all

Laughter as actual medicine

Laugh long
Laugh hard
Until you can't anymore
You must get to the end of your laughter
when it feels a bit dull
Almost like you can't quite recall
what was so funny in the first place.
Do this again and again,
until it doesn't make you feel lost -
this feeling beyond your delight.
So you can begin to know
how much laughing is just
another
nervous tic.

The end

To my homeland,
whoever you are,
you absent parent you -
You pushed your people away from the shore;
Intercepted not when acts were cruel -
to survive
then thrive.

You gained
And reaped and smiled;

Then turned grimly
from the storm
Let loose
When scales snapped free.
And now you look not at me…

I'm too late,
too young in years,
surely,
To be yours.

And I have nowhere to go now.
But
You cannot remove
your connection to it; only stall.

The time will come
When you will take us all
Or take it all.

CHAPTER 3: THE CHILD IN ME

Dust breeze

At this point, I'd really rather be a tree because

then I could just be

stuck, but free. I hear they spend no time at all... talking,

'agendarising'...

And barely observe each other; bent skew, short, or tall. No really,

I've read this - no time at all. Isn't it magical?

A magical thought! And you know what else would finally happen

if I were a tree?

The birds, they'd finally come to me! They'd sit on my branches; I'd look at them,

pecking at me. I'd see them, each cell,

as they nestled - safe,

not knowing, never even thinking about what being there with me

could mean.

I've said 'me' a lot, but the bugs! oh the bugs, also, would

crawl and tickle and munch —

the craziest haircuts they'd give!

I'd just BE there, feeling it all.

How pleasant, this daydream, meditation,

of being a tree.

I've just had a thought - a tree doesn't move... and yet

the activity,

the daily bustle it must see. The things it must feel, like

when a storm comes or

fire breathes.

And the life I would live - so many 100s of years! So many more

than I could dream of, now!

Oh I can't help but think what

it would be

like to

be a tree.

Or a rock. Or

dust on the breeze...

Shadow

Pink dappled ground where the petal leaves fall
Evershade, below
For things so small
But from here: A tree aura on the ground
From out the window
Pulling the mind where it wants to go -
A surprising wish to be less significant
For a bigger immediate world...
For muddy ponds where raindrops pool -
A place of no real wandering interest
for anything else at all.

But what could be better than that
Cool, fresh dew
And nothing of human importance to do...

Rainbath

Rain drools down the window pane -
slips into skeletal cracks;
Drips down jagged spine lines.
Pools below the sill;
Settles inside feet
Splashing against rocky walls.
Droplets work through elbow creases,
Then sprint
'cross knuckled slopes...
Wait a moment; spawn a shiver -
Hang out an open drainpipe.
Wind hits loose,
flung crystals spring -
settle on blades.
Palms spread,
Toes on ice,
Lifting; sludging
off the ground;
Pockmarks left behind.

Cycles

Painted flowers on the wall,
Fallen leaves across the ground below
Swirl in colours, crunching, scraping concrete;
Hiding the bare grey cracks
Pulling apart the clay.
Painted, thinking these fair better;
But in the end, there's nothing to be made
That can surpass the "everness"
Of flowers in the ground.

CHAPTER 4: FINDING TRUTH

Light

God is fractured light -
reflected and tumbling
breaking and entering
Breath on wind.
And just think how
dust lands
On everything
Getting in everywhere
Being never one thing in one place
And always knowing how much
of everything
belongs to it -
Never needing to pull back;
Suck in -
Just knowing it is enough
Because that is the truth of it, no?
That if you know something came from you
Everything about it still exists in you
But you don't have to carry its anything;
None of its feeling,
Or try to refit it back inside -

It's better separated and emitting.

Send it a reminder of the great

spread it belongs to...

Let it feel itself

To sort of say,

Well,

Do as I did

As God did

As breath

Fractured into light...

And let the dust respond to the wind

As and where it is

While you watch

From everywhere,

Waiting -

As light cannot push against wind;

Curious, rather -

Knowing it would land –

To see only where it would land,

Being its witness

As light is

And feeling the wind

As light would.

On a camel's back

I asked God to show me the way
And he said I'd have to go through the eye of a
needle
I said ok
I didn't realise how little space there'd be.
For anything!
How much "letting go",
even,
gets in the way.
He said to put it all down and not look back;
And then asked me why I wondered
Why they burned
When I touched them again.

My family,
friends,
personality, some say,
All got shaved
Like husks
Down the sides
And front

And tops and bottoms and insides and truth and
the whole picture

of my life...

It's hard to talk to people

When you have nothing they find nice

to say.

They still have their husks on.

I start to die to them, melt away.

Leaving behind other flakes I also didn't put
down and leave

In the right place.

And there's no undoing it - I asked for
directions...

To a place I had no clue about.

Saw it in a dream,

Or hallucination -

Did I imagine they were there already?

They kept saying they were -

Did I take a wrong turn?

What makes me sure I didn't?

Where is my certainty?

Or belief in their own way?

There is no denying the feeling of finally-empty hands...

And an empty heart. "Why so empty?" no one asks.

Could it be because of what I filled it with in the first place?

How little I knew of what was meaningful and true!

They always react

When you, or

someone's blue:

Even if in awful ways, the "other" comes alive for you.

And then a hook is in - I wanted more. Didn't you?

That comedian guy, he said it right...

You learn to share in what others' delight.

And that has long been ingrained, destructive,

Skewed.

How far we have travelled.

No wonder it feels like an eye of a needle –

This tiny pinprick in the distance that barely exists

Because no one else is there -

Almost literally!

Such, so that even when you arrive

You feel like you've been dumped in hell because it is so…

sparse!

But when you look up, breathe in, and start to feel

What is now around you… hhhmm…

When I came to -

Correction -

each time I come to,

Because honestly I keep reaching for those pieces

I didn't put down fully yet,

Making more and more of a mess over there,

I am grateful again for how much dying happens in coming here.

Grateful, again, at how much of everything else,

Everyone else,

Cannot come with me.

Because I swear,

I would try and lug it all through.
I do - with my words I try and pull people
through the eye of a needle
And then wonder why they're uncomfortable.

The important ones, I have tried -
and lost them for the pain I caused;
for not seeing how glued to the floor I had been -
that it was me who was ready to move -
While I stood, shoving them.

Truly in awe of how much my own will gets in
the way,
As "good for all" as my intentions might be -
I stand in love with how much I don't have to,
cannot possibly,
be in the driving seat because I, too,
Would wreck this place, eventually,
as humans do.

CHAPTER 5: THE TRUTH

Rebirth

I know you think I'm leaving now,
But don't you think you lost me long ago?
And where this seems like a going away,
It's more of a return...
I wish I knew how to convey to you that,
While you may mourn my soul
And think I've entered the desert,
The heat is behind me
And nothing but light surrounds me.

If you get sad at thinking I'm lost
Please know, that's where I've been
For so long, but now I'm here -
Where I see what has been missing;
Why I never found the love
you so wanted to share with me
of any comfort at all.
Or rather now I know how
to let that go.

I sense you think this is the worst of it
My soul is dying with the goats -

Again I wish I knew how
To show you the true faces of
Former playthings,
How close I danced to the devil
back then, and how I have not died
to all goodness and hope, now,
but have only just been born.

Grieving

When the time comes to say goodbye

And you hold your lips steady,

as the words are metered out,

I wish you'd crumble and spill them all at once!

Let them pour out 'til you realise…

You aren't sad!

You are glad - to have known

the life you gently cradle now,

Hammocked in your politely swaying speech…

All the while the stories were much wilder,

And your heart was much "free-er",

When we were both there -

Living un-sorry,

Daring death,

Laughing off consequence,

Wanting only to feel full,

Permitting each moment to be the last!

But now that the last has come and gone,

You're all sewn up.

Stitched shut.

The whole truth of life as I knew it packed away;

Written into neatly labelled character traits
Worth mentioning.

Burst!
For the heavens' sake -
Shout the truth as we lived it!
Feel the end as we felt the middle and
Say how you really feel.

Time lapse

I can't say any more about it.
There's too much, too heavy, spilling anyway…
So why shape the pouring of the story
While it sits there in full view anyway.
You see the mess it made
But don't look at the weapons used.
It's true…
Because then
Then you have to see, say,
Have to act differently
About why it is, why it looks this way.
Too hard, too much work, too little sway.
But, as heavy as it is,
Contents drain and wash away,
Diluted by the rest of life, and
So it will be that
The end won't have you in it,
In a bad way,
At all,
See?

CHAPTER 6: SEEDING

Below the mist

Somewhere in the mist above
The water's edge
Ripples away
Leaving space for sound
To pilfer through
The hazy view
From down below -
The surface of the ground
Above
And what the sound comes rushing through
Was something never new.

Something old;
Some whispered truth,
Ancient as in me and you;
Ancient as in old as dust
That covers coffins
In graves of long dead soldiers
Fighting feuds
Never meant for them -
Words we should have learnt

'til faces blue.
But what can be learned
From absent minds
Of how to speak or see
Or hear
Or read
Into the sacred scripts of silence and expression?

What can come of a rip in the water's tide
That brings a flood of saving tunes,
From souls' first knowings,
Meant for ancient things
Like me and you?

Voices drift to where I lay…
Silent as the day after death takes over -
Silence broken;
Sleeping quakes,
Brain wakes,
Tries to make
Sense of the rush of voices -
Strange,
A sound that had slipped away —

Foreign,

Scraping against long unfractured moments

That came before

contemplation

Of separation,

Of stillness sought and found…

And the news they brought -

Though so much had passed

That wishes almost lived once more -

Was, again, nothing new;

Indeed,

It was the same old promise

Of a future full of strife

Forgetting to proclaim,

Just as loud, the whispered trail of truth behind

The echoic bite of tumbling words;

That is…

Against all deep truth

We push away;

Carving ourselves from roots.

Shooting shoots.

Back in the soily depths where I lay

I try to release the voices -

Let them slink back

To the heights of the clouds so dreamily far

From the murky misty

Underbelly;

Chosen

Catacomb;

Happily undisrupted.

Could we be a whisper

Tell me again that the wind
Is not a thing, same as you and me -
an entity -
Tell me it chases nothing;
Follows no path
And never turns back on itself
All sudden, like
It hasn't just discovered a new direction
Tell me it doesn't enjoy itself
Its own power
The sensation of twirling
Round and round and round
Eating up the land
And kicking dust
Manically like it's lost its mind -
Or its *self*
For a sweet moment
Of intensity -
Whatever it's feeling -
And then tell me again
How it feels no difference

In rushing in;
Or whispering through…

This to me, cannot be true
The only part I can believe
Is that it doesn't shy the same
Or make itself small the same
And it doesn't concede silly points the same;
The way others might want it to.

Dying to live

It's in trying to hold on to something
that makes us feel anxious,
When all of the cosmos is pulling us to change -
Because we asked it to.
The fear of not knowing ourselves sets in:
What will our lives mean;
What will it have all been for?
Forgetting that we want to leave it behind
for reasons well considered.

It's in not knowing how to accept a void
Because it's not familiar
That we hold tight
to things that have impacted us
in the biggest ways -
Too often, trauma.
Because we have no training
on committing the positive as securely;
To have it mean as much.
It's one of those well considered reasons, so
Hold on to that -

There is no void
There is only the new;
And, sure, it's scary
Because there's no backstory in this,
And innocence is hard
In a world that equates age to worthiness -
We just don't get
that we spend our years here
losing the knowledge we're born with.

Allow the rebirth,
the new story-start,
hold fast
to the knowledge you're arriving with,
believe there's a whole life still ahead -
Greater, still, than that which you leave dead -
If you can accept how small the world
will want to make you feel,
And not have it mean anything real.

Roughage

Searching the banks for that childhood favoured
spot
Was harder than anticipated.
So much changes.
This was back when I was a girl made to feel like
a flower
Waiting to be picked -
And before I understood
That picked things die;
And soon, too.
Before I knew I could become a wild
Rugged creeper in the garden of
Some storybook house
In the mountains
Without a
Sooner death - or
Promise of gifts that can't be given.
Before I registered:
My will was not for tap water,
but wild springs.

But there on the banks,

I had stones to swallow.

Roaming

Back and forth

Looking hard for anything that might have been a
large tree -

to a child's mind -

Growing through a rock

Now fallen,

Perhaps;

I relented and

came home early

Less nostalgic than planned.

Before I understood that happy and nostalgic

seldom co-exist.

I had to give it up

Instead of promising myself

another round of not finding something -

that's only promise is to change -

I only ever thought I wanted

Based on comments

Grown-ups made.

Before I understood that grown-ups

Have always only ever been

Trapped children

Needing to believe; that

Childhood fantasies were

Flowers grown for harvesting;

Gathered to death

Beyond reason or question.

Before I understood that those fantasies

Never really belonged to children at all

But rather to their trapped hopeful parents

Grandparents

Aunts, uncles, family friends,

And other grown-ups who

were only ever asked the same questions,

heard the same comments,

watched the same TV type moments

created by grown-ups that

came before them

and who only ever wanted ideals to matter.

On those banks,

By that favoured stream —

Quiet now, while none should roam,

Except for the horse

Jittering in response to my

Unexpected presence -

I had to shrug

And give it up

To lessons learned -

Allow the stones to scrape my throat clean

and free my heart

to believe that being

a wild garden creeper

was always going to be better

than a flower picked

and waiting to die

in the vase of a home

that may be pretty

but would just as soon be wrecked by absent
hands.

Storybook homes belong to the

Wanderers in the wind.

Storybook lives belong to those

who leave the banks of the stream

and marshal up the next hill

and into the next gorge

to find other things that refuse to die quietly

In glass cases

Looking neat -

Dead petals arranged below -

Rather than gusting wildly,

with happy travelling seeds to spare,

to places flower pickers never venture —

And now that I understand,

I tell myself

that to go back again

must be with the sole purpose

of cutting new paths

For ever more wildlings to go.

Change

You had plans,
dear human; you made them with intent.
And now the reasons are
Debris.
But the path unfolds yet…
You are pushed, propelled forward
In the same way, plans go on,
though the path -
It's not the scenery you expected.
But each ticket is the same.
The walk in the park, the same.
Nullified against the force of it anyway
You fight against all the coming seasons -
The death and the promise of new life;
just as if they were the same.
Vapid -
Mellow, you say.
Tearful at a nudge -
Knife's edge,
All the day.

Seek

Walk through life, little child
Hands in your pockets
Observe
Study everything, little child
Smile on your face
Until
Something halts your stomping
Draws your eye in
Move
Go towards what pulls you
Wills your fingers get involved
Try
Think and tinker long and wearily
If you can
Ask anything of anyone
Fearlessly.
Tssk the unanswered,
Find it out another way...
Seek

Get up

A shook out Earth -

like hazardously smoothed bedding -

Awaits;

folds and creases, wrinkles and pleats, bumps and lumps.

Like an ant scurrying across cotton plains,

Making such small progress,

We trek the almost visible paths -

Up ruffle-hills; down indent-valleys.

We are dust in motion against the scope.

Moving with only a vague sense of purpose,

While grassy plains of satin sheets

don't hold our feet too well.

Rocks, like crumbs, contemplated

and averted.

The comfortable air, like a warmed capsule of a room,

Strokes our arms and tickles our hairs to stand on end.

But we don't barricade our flesh from its reach.

These elements don't exist in images,

And we are here to feel them seep into our cells.

You're already here.

MELISSA ENSLIN was born and raised in South Africa, growing up during the most vital period in the country's history so far. Her education took place at Rhodes University, and her career began as a teacher at a South African high school where she truly fell in love with the specificity and simultaneous ambiguity of poetry, despite having written and published poetry from a much younger age. During these years it became clear to her that the only true super power that exists in the world lies in the way one is able to construct language, which is done often with intention and sadly more often without it. Nothing else has quite the same impact on the minds and souls of others. With a body that craves adventure as much as the soul craves resonance, she now lives in Italy with her husband and dogs, doing mostly regular things; all the while longing for nothing else but quiet time amongst the bugs and weed flowers, because she finds the smaller ecosystems the most savagely captivating. If you have ever felt the need to fall through a crack and meet your soul at its origin, or regain a clear visual on your inner child, you will love her poetry.

(author photo and effects by Claudio De Luca)

www.ingramcontent.com/pod-product-compliance
Lightning Source LLC
Chambersburg PA
CBHW041955090426
42811CB00013B/1495